Barcode in Back

Cover Story

Have You Got What It Takes to Be a Magazine Editor?

by Lisa Thompson

Compass Point Books ✦ Minneapolis, Minnesota

First American edition published in 2009 by
Compass Point Books
151 Good Counsel Drive
P.O. Box 669
Mankato, MN 56002-0669

Editor: Anthony Wacholtz
Designer: Ashlee Suker
Art Director: LuAnn Ascheman-Adams
Creative Director: Joe Ewest
Editorial Director: Nick Healy
Managing Editor: Catherine Neitge
Content Adviser: Lorraine Shea,
            Executive Editor, *Fit Yoga* magazine

Editor's note: To best explain careers to readers, the author has
created composite characters based on extensive interviews and research.

This book was manufactured with paper containing
at least 10 percent post-consumer waste.

Library of Congress Cataloging-in-Publication Data
Thompson, Lisa.
  Cover story : have you got what it takes to be a magazine editor? / Lisa Thompson.
      p. cm.—(On the Job)
  Includes index.
  ISBN 978-0-7565-4080-7 (library binding)
  1. Journalism—Editing—Vocational guidance—Juvenile literature. 2. Periodical
editors—Juvenile literature. I. Title.
  PN4778.P37 2009
  070.4'1—dc22   2008038379

Image Credits: Chien-Min Chung/Corbis, cover (front); DaydreamsGirl/iStockphoto,
11 (top); Ian McDonnell/iStockphoto, 11 (middle left); RickBL/iStockphoto, 11 (middle
right); James Ferrie/iStockphoto, 11 (bottom); Chris Schmidt/iStockphoto, 20; Marcus
Clackson/iStockphoto, 23 (middle), 40 (top); Mandy Godbehear/iStockphoto, 26 (front);
Aldo Murillo/iStockphoto, 37 (middle); Brad Killer/iStockphoto, 40 (bottom);
Wallenrock/Shutterstock, 41 (top). All other images are from one of the following
royalty-free sources: Big Stock Photo, Dreamstime, Istock, Photo Objects, Photos.com,
and Shutterstock. Every effort has been made to contact copyright holders of any
material reproduced in this book. Any omission will be rectified in subsequent printings
if notice is given to the publishers.

Visit Compass Point Books on the Internet at *www.compasspointbooks.com*
or e-mail your request to *custserv@compasspointbooks.com*

Table of Contents

Ready to Go

Up and at it!

8 A.M. Check e-mails

9 A.M. Read through articles

10 A.M. Staff meeting

2 P.M. Radio interview

3 P.M. Meeting with marketing department

Notes • Confirm Max West
• Call accounts
• Get update about Friday photo shoot

It's 8 A.M., and I'm already in the office reading my e-mails. I focus on the ones marked "high priority" because there are too many to read in a single morning. Our regular monthly issue has just gone to the printer, so we've turned our attention to the anticipated special summer issue—an issue that is larger than our regular issues.

Max West, one of the best young photographers around, has confirmed he will do a last-minute fashion shoot. What a relief!

The marketing department has asked for another meeting about the launch party for the summer issue. The theme for the issue is "The Best Summer Ever," so we're hoping to hold a night beach party. We like to throw a theme party with our yearly special issue. It is always eagerly awaited and provides great exposure for our magazine and our advertisers.

I'll organize lots of fun and games for the beach party.

Consumer, trade, and news magazines

Consumer magazines cover anything to do with fashion, gardening, entertainment, cooking, travel, cars, and more. Trade magazines are more specialized and include such topics as aviation, organic farming, and hotel management. News magazines cover current events from around the world. News magazines are usually printed more frequently to stay up-to-date.

Hive Magazine

Hive is a teen lifestyle magazine. It covers everything from music and sports to fashion and entertainment. It also includes special interest features, such as the article on skateboarding we're publishing in the summer issue.

Hive aims to provide cutting edge content (what we include in the magazine) and style (how it looks). Our freelance artists, photographers, writers, and stylists include some of the best young-adult talent you can find.

Our staffers are like bees that travel to all corners of the globe to bring back the freshest, most contemporary stories and images to *Hive*!

My vision for *Hive* is that it should be like an exciting tour around our world—a peek into what's happening for teens everywhere. All our staffers love what they do, and I think that comes across in the quality of *Hive*. The readers seem to love it, too!

We're big on teamwork at Hive

Magazines beat TV

Studies show that, dollar for dollar, magazines are more effective than television at generating brand awareness and product sales. Magazine advertisements can target the audience they want by appearing in specific magazines.

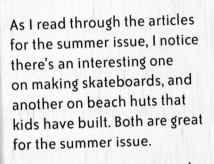

As I read through the articles for the summer issue, I notice there's an interesting one on making skateboards, and another on beach huts that kids have built. Both are great for the summer issue.

There's a huge buzz around the summer issue—and this one is shaping up to be our biggest ever. Our readers and advertisers look forward to it. We always try to do something to make these issues different and exciting. We also have a few surprises in store.

Putting together this issue can take eight months to plan and organize. This is especially stressful because we still have to publish the monthly issues of *Hive* at the same time.

Skateboarding is popular right now.

I'm thinking of ways to incorporate a beach hut into our beach party—it could serve as a changing room.

Cover lines

Cover lines are the small lines of text that appear on a magazine cover to explain what can be found inside.

I make changes and add comments to the articles. At 10 A.M., the meetings start. As the editor in chief, my job involves approving every article, picture, layout, headline, and cover line. I have meetings scheduled with most of the departments—features, art, advertising, and marketing. I also have phone meetings with some of our freelance photographers, stylists, and writers. Something tells me today is going to be a whirlwind of problem-solving and decision-making.

The editor in chief works closely with members of all the departments.

Great article, just needs some small changes— see margin notes.

Inbox
42

Reply
→

Send
☞

Sent
✈

Seen

Get Mail

From: **Stella**
To: **Sally**
Subject: **What a Day!**

Hi Sally,
Here's my chaotic schedule for the rest of the day!

Noon—Match photos with files; confirm and style fashions; approve layouts; contact writers and photographers.

2:00—Meet for an interview at local radio station to promote our new contest—one lucky reader will win an internship with us!

3:00—Meet with the marketers about the launch party.

4:00—Back in office to jot down new ideas for future issues; check layouts for the summer issue.

Radio interviews can be quite daunting, but they are a great way to market Hive.

Sally, one of the editorial assistants, is kept busy all day trying to contact various people.

At 6 P.M., some skateboarding pictures from a photo shoot come in. They look fantastic! This summer issue is certainly taking shape. I'm excited as I leave the office, even though I have a few more feature articles to read at home and a couple of layouts to consider before the morning.

Why People Love Magazines

Magazines are popular because people like the experience of reading them and flipping through the pages. They make them feel more informed. People also see magazine reading as a time to relax and a way to have some time for themselves. We don't need any special technology for magazine reading. We can do it anytime, anywhere, as long as we have light!

Top three

The top three subject categories for magazines are:
1. entertainment/celebrities
2. fashion/accessories
3. food/nutrition

Mag about you!

The worldwide craze over magazines is driven by the wide choice of titles available. They cater to almost every interest, hobby, and activity.

WWW

Market research shows that magazine readers are likely to use the Internet to research topics they read about in magazines. They're also more likely to save magazine pages with Web addresses for future reference.

How I Became a Magazine Editor

Growing up, I never really thought about a career in publishing. There were always lots of magazines at home, though, and I read every one about fashion and music. Mom liked the celebrity news, and dad was into science and gardening magazines. My two older brothers subscribed to magazines about surfing, music, and motorcycles.

Art was one of my favorite subjects at school, and at one stage, I thought about becoming a graphic designer.

I also enjoyed writing, and when I was 14, I won a writing competition sponsored by a magazine. I never imagined I'd end up running one!

PUN FUN

The writer said to the editor, "Proofread carefully to see if I any words out."

After finishing high school, I studied journalism at college, where my interest in photography and reporting grew. After college, I went traveling. I saved for my trip by waitressing, but I constantly sent photos and articles into magazines and local papers to try to get published.

Eventually I landed a job writing entertainment and restaurant reviews for a weekly magazine. I was flying off in all directions, interviewing people and eating yummy food! I did that job for about three years.

I gained a world of experience by traveling. I also learned about food when I was waitressing, which really helped later when I had to write restaurant reviews. At an industry function, I met Kieran Walsh, the publisher of *Hive*. He loves adventure and extreme sports. I've always admired the exciting style of his magazine. It pushes the boundaries both in look and content. It's not a predictable magazine delivering the same thing every issue.

Kieran's love of adventure shines through the style and content of Hive.

Hive likes to inspire, surprise, and amaze its readers. Kieran and I clicked. We shared similar ideas about magazines. It was really inspiring!

One day, as I was about to hop on a plane to New York, I got a call from Kieran offering me a job as the new editor in chief at *Hive*. It was a dream come true. I was nervous and excited by the challenge.

That call was two and a half years ago, and I am still nervous and excited about the challenge of doing every *Hive* issue— particularly the summer issue. This one looks like it will be our best one yet!

An Editor in Chief's Job

Editors in chief are responsible for a magazine's look and content. They are a business manager and journalist rolled into one. They need strong skills in research and communication, and they need to have a love of publishing.

Wearing the business manager's hat

Editors in chief need to understand their market and determine what topics would interest their readers. They must determine how to keep existing readers while attracting new ones.

Editors must also have a solid understanding of the publishing process, a knowledge of business management, and excellent leadership skills. Also, as with most jobs, communication and people skills are a plus.

A big part of being an editor in chief involves business management.

Wearing the journalist's hat

I also lead and manage the editorial team, so I need to have strong analytical skills and a strong vision for the type of articles that appear in the magazine. This is called an editorial strategy. Editing and writing skills—as well as being able to assess written material—are crucial to being a good editor in chief. I must also have a basic understanding of media law—laws that deal with telecommunications (e-mail, multimedia) or printed sources.

A strong team spirit is essential at a magazine publishing company.

Tough calls

The editor in chief makes tough decisions. This means taking credit when things go well, but also taking blame when they don't.

An article that may be controversial can be a major headache for editors in chief. They must carefully consider the consequences before authorizing any article for print. If the editor in chief decides to publish a controversial article, he or she must make sure to include both sides of the issue.

Ten Qualities of Successful Editors

1. An interest in current events and the latest trends

2. An understanding of the readers' interests

3. Self-confidence and the ability to follow your instincts

4. Fearlessness—especially when dealing with advertisers and publishers

5. Stamina—both physical and mental

6. The ability to encourage sensational performances from your staff

7. Strong editorial skills

8. The ability to surround yourself with other talented and knowledgeable people

9. Strong mentor and leadership skills

10. The ability to say "no" when something is not up to standard

Who runs a magazine?

As editor in chief of *Hive*, I report to the publisher. He manages all aspects of the publishing business, including contracts, finance, sales, marketing, and production. The managing editor works for the editor in chief and manages the in-house and freelance feature writers. The creative director is responsible for the overall look of the publication. He or she oversees the branding of the magazine and ensures the image of the magazine matches the editor in chief's vision.

Congratulate staff on a job well done, but know when to ask for more.

Subscribe and save

Subscribing to magazines is usually cheaper than buying each issue at a store (since you get a discount for paying in advance). You also have the convenience of having them delivered to your home. You never have to miss out on your favorite magazine!

Who's Who at *Hive*

The size of a magazine's team depends on the amount of work to be done. The number of issues, as well as the number of pages in each issue, determines how many people are needed to do the work. *Hive* is a thick magazine that comes out every month, so we have many people on our team.

Our magazine is broken up into departments. As editor in chief, it is my job to oversee many departments and roles to ensure the creation of an exciting publication and a healthy business.

The finance department monitors the company's profits, costs, and budget.

Magazine staffers start their morning.

Features department
This department includes a senior writer who writes special-interest pieces for each issue. There's also a features editor who works with freelancers on specific articles.

Fashion, health, and beauty department
The fashion, health, and beauty editor oversees the content. The senior writer writes and articles for this section. Once the writing is near completion, the copy editor checks it for grammar, style, and readability. The proofreader looks over the articles, too, but after it is in layout and has images. There is also an editor's assistant who assists the editor and writer.

Lifestyle department

The lifestyle editor is in charge here. This department includes a sports writer, a music and entertainment writer, and the technology writer. They also have an assistant editor to help them out.

A sports writer in the field

The creative director motivates the design team with original ideas.

Art department

The art department is headed by the creative director, who works with the editor in chief and the production department to come up with the look of each issue. The department includes the art director, a senior designer, and other designers.

Photo department

This department works with the creative director and the art director to find pictures for each issue. A photo editor, photo researcher, and photo research assistant are part of the photo department.

Choices have to be made as to which images to include with each issue.

23

Advertising department

The advertising department finds new advertisers and works to keep existing ones. It includes an advertising director, manager, and coordinator. The amount of advertising sold for each issue often determines the size of each issue.

Marketing and promotions department

The marketing and promotions department works on increasing the profile of the magazine. It also works with the advertising department on special-event promotions and contests. It includes a marketing and promotions director, manager, and coordinator.

Marketing is full of innovative people who love coming up with ideas.

Printing presses

Production department

The production department works with printers and distribution companies to make sure the magazine is produced and delivered on time. It includes a production director and production manager who ensure the department runs smoothly. They may also handle the magazine's circulation, although many magazine companies have a separate circulation department.

Freelancers can be expensive, but they are usually flexible and hardworking.

Freelance contributors

Our pool of talented freelancers sets *Hive* apart from other magazines. Freelancers are creative people who contribute on an issue-by-issue basis, depending on the look and content of a particular issue. Each issue, *Hive* uses different photographers, writers, illustrators, and stylists.

Readers and Research

Who is the average *Hive* reader?

Magazine editors must know and understand their readers. This allows them to decide what kind of stories to publish and what the magazine should look like. Connecting with readers is one of the key factors to increasing sales and producing a successful magazine.

Know your audience

Like other businesses, magazine companies conduct market research to find out what their customers want. This can be done by conducting surveys, test marketing (asking a test group what they think), or encouraging reader feedback.

Hive reader profile

Age: 13–19
Gender: male and female
The *Hive* reader is

- sporty
- fashion-oriented
- optimistic
- tech-savvy
- interested in the news
- curious
- motivated
- a music lover
- creative

Coolhunting

Coolhunting is a modern method of market research—
literally hunting down what is "cool." For magazines,
fashion labels, and music producers, it's important to
know what young people think is the latest, cool thing.
So they hire coolhunters to do research and carry out
undercover "cool" investigations.

Progress Meetings for the Summer Issue

Meeting with the writers

We're including some of our readers' favorite summer memories in the biggest article in the summer issue. It's looking good and reads easily. I think it'll work well for general interest and will delight the readers who contributed!

Our senior features writer, Amy, has almost finished her article on summer sports. She'll have no problem meeting the deadline. We also go through the film and technology reviews.

At the end of the meeting, we decide to add another article about summer music festivals. This issue is going to appeal to all of our readers!

Meeting with the art department

In our next meeting, we go over the layouts, which are beginning to take shape. Some of the advertisers have prepared special ads just for this issue, and they look fantastic.

The layout artists will let the managing editor know if the articles need cutting to fit the layout. This is called copyfitting.

For the most part, everything looks good, but we decide to change some of the fonts used in the layouts. Although they look good, they are too hard to read.

A designer checks the layout before handing it over for our approval.

Meeting with the art and production departments

In our last meeting of the day, we decide to use gold and silver metallic type on the cover. We choose a striking yet simple photo for the cover. The test runs are back from the printer, and the gold type doesn't look like we imagined. After some discussion, we settle on bronze instead. We also decide to run with a mini version of the artwork for the launch party tickets.

PUN FUN A good editor can keep a reader spellbound.

On Location at the Photo Shoot

We are down the coast at a wonderful beach called Dolphin Bay. The models, crew, and photographer—Max West—arrived last night and stayed at a nearby hotel. It's an early start, and they have to be on location before sunrise.

It's still dark outside. The models are getting their hair and makeup done. Because it's a beach theme, the look is natural, but a little make-up and hair styling is still needed.

PUN FUN The photographer was in a hurry because he knew it would be over in a flash.

30

Photo editing

Photo editing is retouching photos to make them more appealing than the originals. This is common practice in magazine publishing, especially with shots of models. Photo editing makes models look younger, slimmer, smoother, and more tanned than in real life. Some people believe this causes self-esteem problems for teenagers, who want to look like people they see in magazines. It is impossible for them to do so because the photos themselves are not real!

Max and his assistant visited the location yesterday to get ideas for the kinds of shots they want. The theme is "golden summer days," so the look is to be dreamy, as though you are remembering the greatest summer day ever.

Max begins taking photographs just as the sun is rising. He takes lots of photos of the beach setting. I know they will be fantastic.

Just as he's taking some photos of surfers, we see the famous dolphins of Dolphin Bay! Max excitedly takes photos of them—perhaps we can use some in our summer issue.

Looks just right!

Stylists work with photographers to organize and arrange shots so that they convey the perfect look and feel.

The stylist is putting the finishing touches to the jewelry that is laid out on shells for close-up photographs. It's important to get all the shots we've planned for, so I constantly refer back to the schedule to make sure we're on track.

We were supposed to break for lunch around noon, but Max wants the models to pose with some of the locals. After lunch, Max runs through all of the planned photos and takes a few shots that were missing. As the sun goes down, the final shots of the series are taken of the entire crew gathered around a beach bonfire.

The models and locals had a great laugh posing for photos!

Back at the hotel we look through the day's work. The photos look awesome. It really looks like a dreamy summer day!

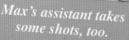

Max's assistant takes some shots, too.

Looking Back— The First Magazines

The word *magazine* was first commonly used in 1731 with the publication of *The Gentleman's Magazine* by Edward Cave. Its aim was to entertain with stories of crime and romance. It was very popular. It was not just sold—it was also rented in hotels, coffee shops, and barber shops. Soon after, *The Lady's Magazine* was published.

Early magazines did not restrict themselves to hobbies and leisure interests. They often had political and religious content. In the mid-1700s, magazines did not always have covers. Many had their cover page as a table of contents or they began an article on the cover. The first teen magazines appeared in America and England in the 1940s.

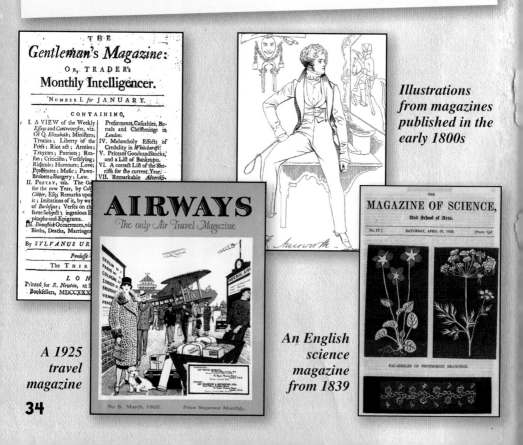

Illustrations from magazines published in the early 1800s

A 1925 travel magazine

An English science magazine from 1839

34

Photography in fashion

Fashion photography was first used in French magazines in the early 1900s. The New York-based *Vogue* magazine also contributed to the beginnings of fashion photography. Its rival, *Harper's Bazaar*, became another leader in using fashion photography. The two magazines were groundbreaking in the field throughout the 1920s and 1930s.

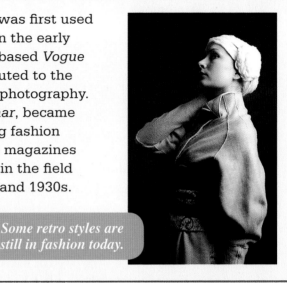

Some retro styles are still in fashion today.

Magazines galore

There's now a magazine for practically every imaginable interest, from fashion or food to football or fishing.

There are more magazines today than ever before. Magazines both inform and entertain. It's this combination that has kept sales rising for nearly 300 years.

The most expensive magazine

Wilmott is a finance magazine based in London that contains cutting-edge research, information about new products, book and software reviews, and in-depth analyses of financial markets. You can buy six issues a year for $800. That's $130 each!

Why Advertisers Love Magazines

Reading a magazine is a relaxing and engaging experience. Statistics show the average reader spends around 45 minutes reading each issue.

Advertisers love magazines because they let them engage with a consumer and they have the reader's full attention. Research shows that most people are more focused when reading a magazine than when watching the television or listening to the radio. That means it is more likely that the reader will remember the ads.

Advertisers can target their market directly. They have a good idea what type of person would buy the magazine. Also, positive experiences with magazines boost the impact of magazine advertising. People often read magazines multiple times and share them with other people, giving the advertisers added exposure.

Ad/Edit ratio

Advertising plays a key role. Depending on the market, advertising brings in about half of a magazine's revenue.

For most weekly consumer magazines, the ratio of advertising pages to editorial pages is generally 45–50 percent advertising to 50–55 percent editorial.

Top three advertising categories for teen magazines:

1. fashion
2. entertainment/ technology
3. food

Making magazines attractive

Many newspapers include free magazines, particularly on weekends. These may be monthly magazines or weekly inserts. Advertising covers the cost to the publisher, and the reader is more tempted to buy the paper because it comes with a free magazine.

Another marketing tool is giving a small free gift with the magazine. The occasional "freebie" lures readers, especially those who may not be regular customers, to buy the magazine.

The Special Issue Takes Shape

Tuesday	Wednesday	Thursday	Friday	Saturday	Sunday
	1	2	3	4	5
8	9	10	11	12	
15	16	17	18	19	
22	23	24	25	26	
29					

The deadline is getting closer, and there is still a lot to do!

Eight days to go

With just over a week until the printer's deadline, layouts have come in from the art department. They are checked and rechecked. There needs to be font changes to some of the photograph captions, but otherwise they are looking good.

We discover that some advertisers have not provided final artwork for their ads. The advertising department gets busy hunting down the missing artwork. Meanwhile, a couple of articles are still missing pictures, so people from the photo department try to track down the photographers.

Calls are made to find the missing pictures.

I do a read-through to make sure all the headings and captions read well. I mark up last-minute changes and corrections.

Proofs of the cover with the revised colors are back for approval. It looks just as I had imagined it. That earlier decision to switch to bronze has paid off.

PUN FUN

The editor realized that to write with a broken pencil is pointless.

Five days to go

I meet with the marketing department for an update on the progress of the launch party. I scan the RSVP list. Most of our big advertisers are coming, as well as many of our freelancers. This is shaping up to be a great party!

Marketing gives me a schedule for the radio and TV interviews. They have me lined up to do several promotions the day the magazine comes out.

At 3 P.M., I head to the all-important meeting with my bosses—the owners of the magazine. They want to hear how the magazine is doing. I've prepared a full presentation. Equipped with statistics and notes, I feel confident in telling them that we'll produce the best summer issue ever.

Three days to go

I just received a surprising phone call. A big-name advertiser—one we've been after for a long time—has suddenly decided they want to place two full-page advertisements in this special issue. I guess they heard through the grapevine that it's going to be huge. This is amazing news, but how am I going to get two spare pages at this short notice?

This is too good an opportunity to miss—I have to make a bold decision. I'm going to move a two-page article on street art to the next monthly issue to slot the new advertiser's pages in. I'll personally call the writer to explain the situation. He has written for us before, so I'm sure he'll understand our constraints.

Two days to go

My assistant tells me we are still missing an advertiser's artwork and the final photos for one article. I'll send some urgent e-mails and make a few firm phone calls. Sally has promised me the missing pictures by tomorrow morning, but I need to know what's happening right now!

One day to go

Long hours for the art department and one final read-through for me. It feels like I've read the magazine 100 times, but I need to make sure everything is just right.

Phew! Those missing images turned up. Everything has been approved, so I'm going to give the final go-ahead to the printer. No matter how organized we are, it always seems like a mad rush for the last few days!

The printer has finally started!

Here It Is!

The special summer issue of *Hive* is finally finished! I am so relieved—the cover looks fantastic! I walk down the street and see it in the newsstands. Is it me, or does that awesome metallic cover really catch the eye? I watch as two people grab copies, have a flip through, and then buy the magazine!

All the work was worth it. It really is the biggest and best summer issue ever! I race back to the office to begin my radio interviews, and then it's a quick sprint to the television station to appear on a TV show for teenagers.

PUN FUN

Pencils could be made with erasers on both ends, but what would be the point?

The launch party

The beach bonfire is lit as the sun sets. We all want to celebrate the success of the summer issue. Our sales are up, and we have also attracted more big-name advertisers. *Hive* just gets bigger and bigger, which is great news for us and our advertisers.

I give a speech thanking all the people who have contributed and congratulate everyone on their hard work. It's a fun night for everyone. Mandy and Dan from the photo department get some great shots so we can share some of the fun in our next issue. Thankfully, tomorrow starts the weekend and I get to sleep in. But on Monday, I will be in the office to begin the next issue. The buzz at *Hive* magazine never stops!

Job Opportunities

Step **1**

Volunteer for the school paper to build your writing and editing skills. Finish school with the best grades you can get, especially in English and art.

Step **2**

Apply to local newspapers or magazines for an evening or summer internship while you are still at school. It may be unpaid, but the experience will be worth it.

Step **3**

Go to college and complete a degree in journalism, English, or mass communications.

'guess guess bas
probably corre
edu·cator
professional
edu·ca·tion ed
training and ins
young people in s

Step **4**

Employers place great emphasis on work experience, so be sure to keep writing. Research magazines so you understand the style of articles they publish. Then you will have a better chance that they will publish the articles you submit.

Since employers value work experience so highly, people generally work their way up from a writer to a features editor—and perhaps an editor in chief position one day.

Doing professional internships once you've finished full-time study can be a huge plus because companies will often hire people they already know.

Now, where did I put that phone message?

You may have to work long hours—especially when deadlines loom—and writers may require careful handling. But seeing the finished product that you have helped create is amazingly satisfying.

Opportunities for editors

There are many related careers for editors:
- other forms of publishing, such as books and newspapers
- digital and online publications (Web sites, e-books)
- copywriting
- freelance journalism

Find Out More

In the Know

- According to the American Society of Magazine Editors, there were 12,797 magazine titles available in the United States in 1989. That number jumped to 19,532 in 2007.

- A new phenomenon is happening in the magazine industry (particularly in Europe): Magazines are being given away free! The advertising income that the publisher receives easily covers the costs of production. This practice is especially popular in Spain.

- The oldest general interest magazine, *The Gentleman's Magazine,* was created for the well-educated public and had articles on politics and poetry. Its last issue was published in 1907.

- As of May 2007, the U.S. Department of Labor estimates that the average hourly wage for an editor is $26.45, equalling $55,020 a year. The lowest 10 percent earned $27,360, and the highest 10 percent earned more than $91,390.

Further Reading

Elliott, Rebecca. *Painless Grammar*. Hauppauge, N.Y.: Barron's, 2006.

Fletcher, Ralph. *How Writers Work: Finding a Process That Works for You*. New York: HarperCollins, 2000.

Gannon, Susan, Suzanne Rahn, and Ruth Anne Thompson, eds. *St. Nicholas and Mary Mapes Dodge: The Legacy of a Children's Magazine Editor, 1873–1905*. Jefferson, N.C.: McFarland, 2004.

Gilbert, Sara. *Write Your Own Article: Newspaper, Magazine, Online*. Minneapolis: Compass Point Books, 2008.

On the Web

For more information on this topic, use FactHound.
1. Go to *www.facthound.com*
2. Choose your grade level.
3. Begin your search.
The book's ID number is 9780756540807
FactHound will find the best sites for you.

Glossary

articles—pieces of writing in newspapers or magazines

branding—overall style and impression of something; the image of a consumer product or service, usually controlled by a marketing department

consumer—person who buys products or services

consumer magazines—magazines that cover broad topics such as fashion, entertainment, or travel

controversial—something that causes a lot of discussion or argument

coolhunting—method of market research that tries to determine what is cool or trendy

cover lines—small lines of text on the cover of a magazine that entice people to buy the magazine

editorial—having to do with editing

features—special articles in a magazine that are intended to stand out and are of special interest

freelancers—people who work for themselves and sell their work to more than one employer

layout—how something is visually arranged

lifestyle—way of living that reflects a person's values, attitudes, and what is important to them

media law—laws that deal with telecommunications or printed sources

mentor—to provide guidance and advice to someone less experienced

photo editing—changing images to make them more appealing

reviews—newspaper or magazine articles that give an opinion on a product such as a book or film

subscribe—to receive something, like a magazine, on a regular basis by paying in advance for a certain period of time or for a set number of issues

trade magazines—magazines that cover specific topics such as fly-fishing, organic farming, or hotel management

Index

Look for More Books in This Series:

Art in Action: Have You Got What It Takes to Be an Animator?

Cleared for Takeoff: Have You Got What It Takes to Be an Airline Pilot?

Creating Cuisine: Have You Got What It Takes to Be a Chef?

Eyes for Evidence: Have You Got What It Takes to Be a Forensic Scientist?

Focusing on Fitness: Have You Got What It Takes to Be a Personal Trainer?

Going Live in 3, 2, 1: Have You Got What It Takes to Be a TV Director?

Trauma Shift: Have You Got What It Takes to Be an ER Nurse?

Trendsetter: Have You Got What It Takes to Be a Fashion Designer?

Wild About Wildlife: Have You Got What It Takes to Be a Zookeeper?